ABOVE ALL ELSE, GUARD YOUR HEART!

Why We Do What We Do

How We Can Change

Wisdom from Proverbs 4:23

LYNN STUHR

ISBN 979-8-88832-204-8 (paperback)
ISBN 979-8-88832-205-5 (digital)

Christian Faith Publishing
832 Park Avenue
Meadville, PA 16335
www.christianfaithpublishing.com

Printed in the United States of America

CONTENTS

The Premise of This Study

Before you begin this study, it's important to grasp the basic premise of this guide. It is found in Romans 7:18–24a of the Amplified Bible. This study will help answer the question asked in the last verse below.

"For I know that nothing good lives in me, that is, in my flesh *[my human nature, my worldliness—my sinful capacity]*.

For the willingness *[to do good]* is present in me, but the doing of good is not.

For the good that I want to do, I do not do, but I practice the very evil that I do not want.

But if I am doing the very thing I do not want to do, I am no longer the one doing it *[that is, it is not me that acts]*, but the sin *[nature]* which lives in me.

So I find it to be the law *[of my inner self]*, that evil is present in me, the one who wants to do good!

For I joyfully delight in the law of God in my inner self *[with my new nature]*,

but I see a different law and rule of action in the members of my body *[in its appetites and desires]*, waging war against the law of my mind and subduing me and making me a prisoner of the law of sin which is within my members.

Wretched and miserable man that I am! Who will *[rescue me and]* set me free from this body of death *[this corrupt, mortal existence]*?"

Paul, an Apostle of Christ

CHAPTER

 **1** 

WHY WE DO WHAT WE DO

EVER WONDER WHY we do what we do? Especially when what we do doesn't make sense or doesn't fit the vision we have of ourselves?

Have you ever made comments like any of the following:

- I don't know why I said that!
- I can't believe I did that!
- What was I thinking?
- That's not me! I'm just stressed!

In different times and situations, we can find ourselves uttering similar, baffling statements of disbelief. The Bible has a very simple explanation as to why we do what we do.

In the New International Version (NIV) Proverbs 4:23, we read, "Above all else, guard your heart, for everything you do flows from it."

In Luke 6:45 (NIV), we also read, "A good man brings good things out of the good stored up in his heart, and an evil man brings out evil things from the evil stored up in his heart. For the mouth speaks what the heart is full of."

According to God's Word, we simply do what is in our spiritual hearts. Good content yields good things and bad content yields bad things. What the spiritual heart takes in, it will send out. Just like the well-known computer lingo, "Garbage in, garbage out." So, when

1

we find ourselves saying and doing things that harm others and ourselves, God says it is because we harbor bad content in our hearts.

The Bible also makes it very clear that guarding our hearts is an ongoing, critical duty we need to do. In Proverbs 4:23a (NIV), the verse begins with, "Above all else guard your heart." Why does God say *"Above all else,* guard your heart?" God says everything we do flows from our hearts. Every feeling, thought, word, and action flows out of our hearts. Over a period of time, the accumulation of our actions make up our lives. Good actions add up to a good life. Bad actions add up to a bad life. In simple terms, the contents of our hearts lead to our thoughts, our thoughts lead to our actions, and our actions determine the quality of our lives.

A Simple Diagram of How Our Natural,
Spiritual Hearts Function

Contents—> Thoughts —> Actions —> Quality of life

Yet when we hear and see this basic Biblical explanation, we may question if it applies to us. Especially if what we do does not fit our view of the kind of people we believe we are. Often, we deny or excuse our bad behaviors. We do not want to believe we are people with bad hearts because of a few inconsistent bad behaviors. After all, other people are the bad people—right? Denial of what God says is true about us, is in fact, from our hearts as well. Remember, everything we do flows from our hearts, even our self-beliefs. What we believe about ourselves will affect our lives and the lives of those around us. So if we want positive outcomes in our lives, we need to store up good in our hearts and keep the bad content out. If the bad does gets in, we need to recognize it and remove it. As we will learn later, recognizing and removing the bad content in our hearts is not an easy task for us to do for ourselves.

Questions for reflection

- Our spiritual hearts continually take in and store up contents, either good or bad. How does this process happen in our daily lives?
- Everything we do flows from the contents of our spiritual hearts. How do we guard our hearts for good content and keep the bad out?

2

WHY WE DON'T DO WHAT WE SHOULD DO

EVER WONDER WHY we don't do what we should do? Especially if we know what we should do is good for us and others? Failing to do what is good is really senseless! Yet at times, we often fail to do what we know we should. Why?

Have you ever caught yourself saying things like any of the following:

- I'll do it, but not right now!
- I know it's important. I promise—I won't forget!
- I'm sorry. It just slipped my mind. I really did want to help!
- I'm sorry. I just didn't have the heart to do it.

These statements do indeed show that we at times fail to do what we should—but again, why?

The last comment above about not having the *heart* to do it gets close to answering the question. In Ezekiel 20:16 (NIV), we again see a simple explanation, it says, "because they rejected My laws and desecrated My sabbaths, for their hearts were devoted to their idols." In chapter 1 of this book, we learned we do whatever is in our hearts.

Now in this Ezekiel verse, God provides an additional fact regarding the functioning of our natural hearts. We fail to do what we should because our hearts, first and foremost, serve our idols. In simple terms, if something we should do isn't really important to us, it will be trumped by content that we really value or *treasure*, even if it hurts us or others!

In chapter 1, we learned there are sins of commission, and now we realize there are also sins of omission. We omit to do what we should do because our hearts serve what we treasure.

In Luke 12:34 (NIV), God tells us something very similar to the Ezekiel passage: "For where your treasure is, there your heart will be also." If we wonder why we don't do what we should, then all we need to do is to look at what we do. We spend our lives doing things our hearts treasure, whether helpful or not for us. It's how our inherited spiritual hearts function.

Questions for reflection

- The contents of our sin-nature hearts can become treasures, which we devotedly serve. Why do our natural hearts have and serve their treasures?
- What would happen in our daily lives if God becomes a treasure in our hearts?
- How can God become the treasure of our sin-nature hearts?

3

GOD'S CONCERN FOR OUR HEARTS

Is GOD CONCERNED about our spiritual hearts? If so, why would a holy, almighty, powerful God be concerned with our sinful, feeble, spiritual hearts?

In 1 Samuel 16:7b (NIV), we see that God does have a real concern for our hearts: "The Lord does not look at the things people look at. People look at the outward appearance, but the Lord looks at the heart."

Why does God look at our hearts? In the New Living Translation (NLT) Proverbs 27:19, we see the answer, "As a face is reflected in the water, so the heart reflects the real person."

The fact that God looks at our hearts, clearly shows his concern for our hearts. When He looks inside our hearts, He sees the kind of people we really are: people who love Him, people indifferent or opposed to him. Though we may be able to fool ourselves and others, God is never fooled. Our spiritual hearts always show God who we really are!

But again, why is an almighty God so concerned with our spiritual hearts? We find the answer in the book of Jeremiah 17:9, The Living Bible Version (TLB), which says, "The heart is the most deceitful thing there is and desperately wicked. No one can know how bad it really is."

The New Life Version (NLV) expresses the verse in a slightly different manner that says, "The heart is fooled more than anything else, and is very sinful. Who can know how bad it is?"

In this verse, God's descriptions of our sin-nature hearts are far from flattering. He uses the terms deceitful, wicked, fooled, sinful, and bad beyond anyone's knowledge! Wow! No wonder God has such concern for our hearts! Our hearts, though feeble compared to God's power, are capable of doing serious evil.

How can such a human, defective thing be capable of causing such evil? The Biblical versions above lead with the words *deceitful* and *fooled*. So, who gets deceived or fooled, and how? We regularly get fooled by our hearts. How do our hearts fool us? Our hearts use a sin thermometer. Our hearts measure ourselves and others by the numbers of sins and by the degrees of evil within those sins. The more sins or the greater the evil of the sins, the more evil we or others become in our eyes. In addition, our sin-nature hearts deceive us to see evil in others but not much in ourselves. Just as God says in Luke 6:42a (NIV): "How can you say to your brother, 'Brother, let me take the speck out of your eye,' when you yourself fail to see the plank in your own eye?"

We can see an example of the sin thermometer at work in Luke 18:10–11 (NLT):

> "Two men went to the Temple to pray. One was a Pharisee, and the other was a despised tax collector. The Pharisee stood by himself and prayed this prayer, 'I thank you, God, that I am not like other people—cheaters, sinners, adulterers. I'm certainly not like that tax collector!"[a]

Clearly, the pharisee's heart has fooled him. His heart measured the degrees of perceived evil. His words could be rephrased as follows: "Thank you God, that my sins are not as bad as his or those other evil doers!"

---

a. <u>18:11</u> Some manuscripts read *stood and prayed this prayer to himself.*

When we say such things, it simply shows God and those around us the degrees of our pride. God does not use a sin thermometer. He sees all sins as evil. In His eyes, hate can be the same as murder. According to Luke 6:42, we can have a Pharisee's heart capable of fooling us to view ourselves better than others even though we all inherit sin-nature hearts.

When our hearts have fooled us, our behaviors are ugly, prideful, and hurtful to others and to ourselves. If someone tries to help us see that our hearts have fooled us, then our hearts also prompt us to become defensive and cause us to deny the truth. If we are able to see that our hearts have fooled us, we need to examine the contents of our hearts. Somehow, bad content got in, and we need to remove it immediately!

Questions for reflection

- God looks inside to see the people we have become while people around us look at our outside. Why are our hearts so revealing to God, yet not so easily seen by ourselves and others?
- God describes our hearts as deceptive, and we are the ones most deceived by our hearts. How can we know when our hearts have deceived us?
- Why do we seldom want to admit to possessing hearts that are so bad that God said it is not knowable how wicked our natural spiritual hearts really can be?
- Why is admitting to God's truth that we each inherit wicked, evil hearts from our births, so important to live lives pleasing to Him after our salvation?

4

MORE HEART FACTS

IN CHAPTER 1, we learned that we do what is in our hearts. In chapter 2, we learned we first and foremost do what we idolize or treasure in our hearts, whether good or bad. Our heart treasures can prevent us from doing what we know we should do.

Knowing that our hearts can cause us such serious troubles, we need to be aware of all the realities of our hearts. What follows is a list of common facts we need to know in order to be able to guard our hearts properly.

Natural Heart Fact Number 1

Our sin-nature hearts continually take in content and harbor what we treasure; things like money, possessions, positions, power, image, pride, status, and success, to identify a few.

Natural Heart Fact Number 2

Our sin-nature hearts will cause us to treat and addictively serve the contents of our hearts as idols. For image, we'll find ourselves lying. For money, we'll steal. For position or status, we'll climb over and hurt others. For power, we may even kill. Our hearts can cause us to do anything to serve the treasures of our hearts.

Natural Heart Fact Number 3

Our sin-nature hearts are extremely bad. In fact, it's not knowable how bad our hearts can be! Therefore, it is difficult, if not impossible, for us to do good even if we have the desire to do good. We read in Romans 7:18 (NIV): "For I know that good itself does not dwell in me, that is, in my sinful nature. For I have the desire to do what is good, but I cannot carry it out."

Natural Heart Fact Number 4

Our sin-nature hearts deceive or fool us and cause us to deny the truth. We don't have idols. We don't really have bad hearts. The hearts of others are far worse! Our hearts can even cause us to claim that we honor God, while the very opposite is true.

"These people honor Me with their lips but their hearts are far from Me." (Matthew 15:8 NIV)

Natural Heart Fact Number 5

Our sin-nature hearts (void of God's help) can't guard themselves from bad contents. The natural state of our hearts, from our births, is depravity. Hearts in a depraved state are attracted to and welcome in bad content!

Okay, time out, please!

So far, everything I've read has been so negative and depressing. I really don't like learning that I possess a deceitful, wicked heart! Where is this study leading?

In the Message version of Proverb 15:15 (MSG), you'll discover just where this book is leading: "A miserable heart means a miserable life, a cheerful heart fills the day with song." We desire meaningful and enjoyable lives. The contents of our hearts lead to our lives being either miserable or cheerful, in service to God or to ourselves. If we actually do guard our hearts above all else, and for only good content, then our lives will be good too.

Questions for reflection

- Do any listed heart facts seem too hard to accept? If so which ones?
- Why can't we trust ourselves to guard our hearts from bad content?
- Think about the times when you have been either miserable or cheerful. What was going on inside?

CHANGING THE FOCUS

SO FAR WE have been primarily self-focused on our sinful hearts. Let's change the focus by considering a different set of questions. Does God have a heart? If so, how would you describe His heart? If God has a heart, can we have hearts like His? If we had hearts like God's, would our lives be different?

To answer these questions, let's consider another set of verses:

> "When the Lord God saw the extent of human wickedness, and that the trend and direction of men's lives were only towards evil, He was sorry He had made them. It broke His heart." (Genesis 6:5–6 TLB)

> "But God removed Saul and replaced him with David, a man about whom God said, 'I have found David son of Jesse, a man after My own heart. He will do everything I want him to do.'" (Acts 13:22 NLT)

> "For God so loved the world that that He gave His only begotten Son, that whosoever believeth in Him shall not perish, but have everlasting life." (John 3:16 KJV)

God certainly does have a heart. He said so. The fact that He sent Jesus, His only Son, to redeem us from eternal hell shows He really does have a heart and that we are the treasures of His heart. A partial list of words to describe God's heart include: loving, forgiving, understanding, compassionate, patience, protecting, and generous. If we had hearts like God's (even just a little), it would certainly result in our lives being very different.

Remember how God describes how our hearts function. The contents in our hearts lead to our thoughts, and our thoughts lead to our actions. Over time, the accumulation of our actions makes up the quality of our lives. If we had the contents of God's heart in our hearts, our lives would reflect God's heart. A heart of divine love. Therefore, having God's love in our hearts would mean we would reflect His love for Him and others.

But is it possible to have the contents of God's heart in our hearts? In 2 Peter 1:3–4 (NIV), we see the answer:

> "His divine power has given us everything we need for a godly life through our knowledge of him who called us by his own glory and goodness. Through these he has given us his very great and precious promises, so that through them you may participate in the divine nature, having escaped the corruption in the world caused by evil desires."

Yes, we can have hearts like God's! He promised that we could. Only God knows how our lives would be different! But we certainly can imagine some changes; more helping, giving, forgiving, and loving like Christ.

But how can we have hearts like God? In the following verses, we read:

> "But the Advocate, the Holy Spirit, whom the Father will send in My name, will teach you

all things and will remind you of everything I have said to you." (John 14:26 NIV)

"For we know how dearly God loves us, because He has given us the Holy Spirit to fill our hearts with His love." (Romans 5:5b NLT)

"I have hidden your word in my heart that I might not sin against You." (Psalm 119:11 NIV)

"For if you live according to the flesh, you will die; but if by the Spirit you put to death the misdeeds of the body, you will live." (Romans 8:13 NIV)

When we are saved, God, the Holy Spirit comes to abide in our hearts. He uses God's Word that we read and His power to change the contents of our hearts to be the contents of God's heart. With the Spirit's help, our hearts then generate thoughts like God's, then God-pleasing actions. Over time, the accumulation of God-pleasing actions leads to God-pleasing lives.

Questions for reflection

- God does have a heart. How can we know the contents of His heart?
- How do we go about possessing spiritual hearts like God's?
- God said we have everything we need to live lives that please Him. If we are born with sin-nature hearts, how can we live lives that please Him?

 **6** 

ABOUT THE HOLY SPIRIT

BEFORE LEARNING HOW the Holy Spirit changes our natural hearts, we need to know more about Him. The following lists detail important facts from the Bible about the Holy Spirit.

Key Attributes of the Holy Spirit

1. He is a supreme, personal being, not an it or some mystical force.
2. He is a coequal, Godhead member of the Triune God.
3. He is a Holy God, usually in an invisible form.
4. He is omniscient, all-knowing about everything.
5. He is omnipotent, all-powerful, able to do anything.
6. He is omnipresent, able to be present everywhere at the same time.

Key Descriptive Titles Ascribed to the Holy Spirit in the Bible with Explanations

1. Advocate—pleads on our behalf to God the Father.
2. Teacher—imparts wisdom, knowledge, and guidance.
3. Helper or Enabler—provides assistance to us in multiple forms.

4. Comforter—brings assurance and peace in our lives.
5. Author—inspired men of God to write the Bible.

Key Duties Mainly Preformed by the Holy Spirit

1. Teaches us about the soul-saving work of Jesus, God the Son.
2. Convicts our hearts of our sins and our need for Christ's salvation.
3. Imparts to us faith in Christ, then keeps us in faith until we enter heaven.
4. Seals us and comforts us with His assurance about our salvation.
5. Abides in us and empowers us to overcome our sinful natures.
6. Enables us to be used by Christ to save the souls of others.

Here are a few examples of the Holy Spirit's presence and power during different events of Biblical history:

At creation. "In the beginning God created the heavens and the earth. Now the earth was formless and empty, darkness was over the surface of the deep, and the Spirit of God was hovering over the waters." (Genesis 1:1–2 NIV)

At the birth of Isaac (when Sarah was very old). "Just as Ishmael, the child born by human efforts, persecuted Isaac, the child born by the power of the Holy Spirit." (Galatians 4:29b NLT)

When Samson fought the Philistines. "As he (Samson) approached Lehi, the Philistines came toward him shouting. But the Spirit of the Lord came powerfully upon him. The ropes on his arms became like charred flax, and the bindings dropped from his hands. Finding a fresh jawbone of a donkey, he grabbed it and struck down a thousand men." (Judges 15:14–16 NIV)

During the life of John the Baptist. "But the angel said to him, 'Do not be afraid, Zacharias, because your petition was heard, and your wife Elizabeth will bear you a son, and you will name him John. You will have great joy and delight, and many will rejoice over his birth, for he will be great and distinguished in the sight of the Lord; and will never drink wine or liquor, and he will be filled with and empowered to act by the Holy Spirit while still in his mother's womb.'" (Luke 1:13–15 AMP)

Later, we learn what Jesus said about John, "I assure you and most solemnly say to you, among those born of women there has not risen anyone greater than John the Baptist;" (Matthew 11:11a AMP).

At the incarnation of Jesus. "How will this be," Mary asked the angel, "since I am a virgin?" The angel answered, "The Holy Spirit will come on you, and the power of the Most High will overshadow you." (Luke 1:34–35a NIV)

At the baptism of Jesus. "As soon as Jesus was baptized, He went up out of the water. At that moment heaven was opened, and He saw the Spirit of God descending like a dove and alighting on Him." (Mathew 3:16 NIV)

At the temptation of Jesus. "Jesus, full of the Holy Spirit, left the Jordan and was led by the Spirit into the wilderness, where for forty days He was tempted by the devil." (Luke 4:1–2a NIV)

During the miracles of Jesus. "But if it is by the Spirit of God that I drive out demons, then the kingdom of God has come upon you." (Matthew 12:28 NIV)

During the crucifixion of Jesus. "How much more, then, will the blood of Christ, who through the eternal Spirit offered himself unblemished to God," (Hebrews 9:14a NIV)

At the resurrection of Jesus and others who believe in Him.

"And if the Spirit of Him who raised Jesus from the dead is living in you, He who raised Christ from the dead will also give life to your mortal bodies because of His Spirit who lives in you." (Romans 8:11 NIV)

At Pentecost. "When the day of Pentecost came, they were all together in one place. Suddenly a sound like the blowing of a violent wind came from heaven and filled the whole house where they were sitting. They saw what seemed to be tongues of fire that separated and came to rest on each of them. All of them were filled with the Holy Spirit and began to speak in other tongues as the Spirit enabled them." (Acts 2:1–4 NIV)

At the salvation of the first Christians. "Peter replied, 'Repent and be baptized, every one of you, in the name of Jesus Christ for the forgiveness of your sins. And you will receive the gift of the Holy Spirit. The promise is for you and your children and for all who are far off—for all whom the Lord our God will call.' With many other words he warned them; and he pleaded with them, 'Save yourselves from this corrupt generation.' Those who accepted his message were baptized, and about three thousand were added to their number that day." (Acts 2:38–41 NIV)

Notice from the examples above how much the Holy Spirit was involved in Jesus' earthly life. As followers of Christ, shouldn't we also desire the Holy Spirit to be involved in our lives?

Questions for reflection

- Reading this chapter may have changed your view of the Holy Spirit. If so, how did your view change?
- The Holy Spirit was involved powerfully in Jesus' earthly life. Why do you think Jesus had the Holy Spirit so involved?
- God desires His Spirit to be involved in our lives. Why should the Holy Spirit be involved in our lives?
- How does the Holy Spirit become involved in our lives?

The Liberation of Our Hearts

Liberation! What a great sounding word! But what does liberation mean? Liberation is the act of setting someone free from imprisonment, slavery, or oppression. The liberation of our hearts and lives is what God does and continues to do for us daily.

How Did God Liberate Us?

We find the answer in the Living Bible version of Romans 6:6–8 and 11 (TLB). "Your old evil desires were nailed to the cross with Him; that part of you that loves to sin was crushed and totally wounded, so that your sin-loving body is no longer under sin's control, no longer needs to be a slave to sin; for when we are deadened to sin you are freed from all its allure and its power over you. And since your sin-loving nature died with Christ, we know that you will share His new life. So look upon your old sin nature as dead and unresponsive to sin, and instead to be alive to God, alert to Him, through Jesus Christ our Lord."

God liberated us when He sent Jesus to pay the debt we owed for all our sins past, present, and future. Jesus paid our debt with His precious blood shed on the cross. His payment set us free from our sin-loving nature and the huge debt it generated by all our sins. In Biblical times, when debtors could not pay their debts, they were jailed until their debts got repaid. Likewise, when we cannot pay the debt we owe God, he sentences us to jail (hell) eternally. Why does God give us an eternal sentence without Christ as our Savior?

Our debts are so severe we can never repay them! Liberation or freedom is usually appreciated or cherished in direct proportion to the size of debt paid for us. A debt the size of a temporary jail sentence isn't appreciated nearly as much as a debt so large (a life sentence) that it can never be repaid. Jesus willingly paid our huge debts for us with His perfect life. When we understand the price Christ paid for us, we'll cherish our freedom and Him for all eternity.

How Does God Continue to Liberate Us?

In the Amplified version we read. "But I say, walk habitually in the [Holy] Spirit [seek Him and be responsive to His guidance], and then you will certainly not carry out the desire of the sinful nature [which responds impulsively without regard for God and His precepts]." (Galatians 5:16 AMP)

God liberates us every time His Holy Spirit overpowers our sinful, natural hearts. Yes, there is a continual battle going on inside us between good and evil—the Holy Spirit and our sinful nature. Which one wins? The one we feed and cooperate with. The Spirit's work within us is not a one-time occurrence. Christ died and rose to liberate us once for our salvation. After our salvation, the Spirit liberates us repeatedly, sometimes, multiple times a day. How does this continual liberation happen?

When we ask (surrender to) the Holy Spirit to lead (triumph) over our sinful hearts, He not only sets us free to live God-pleasing lives, He also empowers us to do so. On our own, we are at the mercy of our deceitful, wicked hearts. Though our sins have been forgiven through faith in Christ, we still have to contend with our sinful hearts until death.

The Spirits' liberation during our lives can continually occur if we yield to His leadership and power. Remembering that the degree of appreciation for liberation is in direct proportion to the freedom received, then, multiple, daily, and lifelong liberations should warrant our lifelong appreciation as well, in addition to our salvation liberation by Christ. Understanding how God liberates us from our deceptive, wicked hearts is certainly the key to living liberated Christlike lives!

Questions for reflection

- What value should the liberation of our hearts by Christ's death and resurrection have to us?
- What value should the Holy Spirit's daily liberation of our sinful hearts have to us?
- Why would anyone choose to refuse such wonderful liberations by God?

THE NEED FOR LIBERATED HEARTS

OKAY! HEART LIBERATION is no doubt feel-good news, but do we really need it? Isn't it just helpful information to know? If we have a saving relationship with Christ, isn't that all we really need? To be saved—yes. To be saved and able to live lives for Christ—no. Consider what the apostle Paul said to the Galatian Christians about living their lives after salvation without the Holy Spirit:

> "You foolish Galatians! Who has bewitched you? Before your very eyes Jesus Christ was clearly portrayed as crucified. I would like to learn just one thing from you: Did you receive the Spirit by the works of the law, or by believing what you heard? Are you so foolish? After beginning by means of the Spirit, are you now trying to finish by means of the flesh?" Galatians 3:1–3 (NIV)[a]

Paul makes it very clear that the Galatians were foolish for thinking they could live their lives in Christ, without the power of the Holy Spirit. Therefore, heart liberation is not only necessary for our salvation but also for our daily lives. Our human efforts under

---

a. Galatians 3:3 in contexts like this, the Greek word for *flesh (sarx)* refers to the sinful state of human beings, often presented as a power in opposition to the Spirit.

the control of our sin-nature hearts can't save us from an eternal hell. Nor can our human willpower enable us to live lives for God after salvation. In both situations, we need the Holy Spirit's power within us to come to saving faith in Christ and to living God-pleasing lives after salvation.

Yes, heart liberation is necessary. Trying to live godly lives without the Holy Spirit is a lost cause before we start. We need the Holy Spirit's power to overcome the evil within before, at, and after our salvation.

Questions for reflection

- Why is the liberation of our natural spiritual hearts necessary?
- Do most Christians know that the Holy Spirit can daily liberate their hearts?
- Do you believe most Christians are satisfied just to be liberated by Christ only?

9

STAGES OF HEART LIBERATION

CERTAINLY, THERE ARE Christians fully aware of God's liberation work in their spiritual hearts. However, some Christians may be unaware of the all stages involved. As a result, some may feel confused about how they can live a Christian life after salvation. Below is God's life long liberation (or enabling) process, listed in stages, with key descriptive features.

Pre-Liberation: The spiritual heart before salvation

- A 100% sin-nature heart inherited from parents at birth
- Describe by God as "wicked" which often deceives the owner
- Thoughts, speech and actions are controlled by the sin-nature heart
- Often includes a "good person" (fooled) vision of self without a need for God

Initial Liberation Stage 1: The moment
of salvation (Justification)

- A spiritual rebirth known as being "born again", 100% accomplished by God

- The Holy Spirit uses the Word to create conviction for the need of salvation by Christ
- A saving faith in Jesus is imparted into the heart of the sinner by the Holy Spirit
- 100% forgiven for all sins past, present and future without any personal merit or cost
- A non-controlling wicked spiritual heart crushed by Christ but still present until death
- A view of self as a Christian, a forgiven child of God and in daily need of God

Growth Liberation Stage 2: Life after salvation (Sanctification)

- Becoming "Christlike" involving God's Word and the work of the Holy Spirit
- Enabled to surrender and cooperate with the will of God by the Holy Spirit
- Christ accomplishes God's will through the Christian via His indwelling Spirit

Final Liberation Stage 3: Heaven after death
or at Christ's return (Transformation)

- 100% accomplished by God in a "tinkly of an eye"
- A 100% transformed "holy" nature with a new "heavenly suited" body like Christ's
- Everlasting love, peace and joy lived with God without tears, sorrows or pains

From the list above we can clearly see the supernatural wonders of our Triune God's liberating works in our spiritual hearts, before, during, and after salvation. Without God's works we simply cannot live a Christian life. With God's works, we are enabled to live with Him and for Him, eternally! Jesus shared these truths when He told us we *"can do nothing without Him"* (John 15:5 NLT), but with Him we *"can do all things"* (Phil. 4:13 NLV).

Questions for reflection

- What thoughts come to mind as you read through the liberation stages of our hearts?
- How would you explain to another Christian what needs to occur in our lives in to order to be able to live a Christian life while on earth?

10

PROOF OF LIBERATED HEARTS

ONE OF THE reasons non-Christians cite for rejecting Christianity is they don't see any differences in the lives of Christians they know. In their defense, some Christians have retorted a cute statement *Christians aren't perfect; we're just forgiven.* Though the statement is true, shouldn't non-Christians see some visible differences in the lives of Christians? If so, what differences should they see?

Early church history may provide some helpful insights. In the book of Acts, we see that the first Christians readily sold their properties and shared the proceeds with others in need. The apostles repeatedly risked threats of prison, beatings, and death when told to stop preaching about Christ. Some non-Christians even risked death to become Christian because they were so desirous of the deep love Christians showed to others.

In the book of James, chapter 1:26–27 (NIV), we find more insights. "Those who consider themselves religious and yet do not keep a tight rein on their tongues deceive themselves, and their religion is worthless. Religion that God our Father accepts as pure and faultless is this: to look after orphans and widows in their distress and to keep oneself from being polluted by the world."

Yes, there should be visible differences in the lives of Christians. We should be seen helping those in need. We should be seen guarding our hearts from the polluting influences of the world. So how can these diffences occur in us? We see the answer in Galatians 5:22–23 (NLT). "But the Holy Spirit produces this kind of fruit in our lives: love, joy, peace, patience, kindness, goodness, faithfulness, gentleness and self-control. There is no law against these things!" In other words, when we surrender to the Holy Spirit's control, *He produces the differences others see in our lives.*

However, if we resist the Holy Spirit's work within us, be aware, there is a default reality! We revert immediately to being led by our sin-nature hearts. Then, our hearts produce fruits of anger, jealousy, hatred, fear, anxiety, and hostility, to list a few. No doubt, the fruits of the Spirit are far more desirable! Sadly, when we resist the Holy Spirit, we also resist receiving His fruits as well.

Yes, Christians aren't perfect, and we are forgiven. But the Holy Spirit can liberate our hearts so that others can see the love of Christ in us, just as the early Christians were known for such amazing and genuine love for others.

Questions for Reflection

- There should be differences non-Christians can see in the lives of Christians. How is the Holy Spirit key for the differences to appear in the lives of Christians?
- How are the fruits of the Holy Spirit God's divine love?
- What would happen if Christians regularly showed the fruits of the Holy Spirit in their lives?
- What do you think the phrase "settled for salvation only" means?
- How would you describe a Christian not settled for salvation only?

11

LIVING WITH LIBERATED HEARTS

IN JOHN 10:10b (AMP), Christ said, "I came that they may have *and enjoy life, and have it in abundance [to the full, till it overflows]."* The Holy Spirit's work within us is key to how we are able to experience the abundant life Christ came to give us. But how does it happen? In Galatians 4:4–6 (NLT), we see when and how it happens: *"But when the right time came, God sent his Son, born of a woman, subject to the law." God sent him to buy freedom for us who were slaves to the law, so that he could adopt us as his very own children. And because we are his children, God has sent the Spirit of his Son into our hearts, prompting us to call out, "Abba, Father".*

The beginning point of the abundant life is at the moment of our salvation. When we hear the Gospel of Christ (which the Holy Spirit impresses upon our hearts), and we believe Christ paid the price for all our sins to save us (which the Holy Spirit enables by imparting faith), that is when God the Holy Spirit enters our hearts.

At that very moment, the Triune God becomes a treasure in our hearts. Remember how our hearts function regarding our treasures. Our hearts always serve our treasures. But this Godhead treasure is different. In Philippians 2:13 (TLB), we discover how God the Holy Spirit is different than any other treasure, *"For God is at work within you, helping you want to obey him, and then helping you do what he wants."* Notice that the Holy Spirit helps us want to please Him. And He gives us the power to do so.

Normally, treasures or idols don't *help* us serve them. Idols usually demand we serve them without their help, even to the point of our harm! Notice also that even with the Spirit's help, we still need to do the service or action. However, if we read God's Word, cooperate with his promptings, use his infused strength, and then actually guard our hearts (with His power)—we think Godly thoughts, which lead to Godly actions that result in Godly living. Not perfect living, but living that serves, honors, and glorifies God.

The keyword for Godly living is *help*. To be helped, we need to cooperate with the Helper. And what does it mean to cooperate with the Holy Spirit? We surrender our will to His. We submit to His leadership and guidance (promptings). We read God's Word, and the Spirit teaches us what we need to know. We can even ask God the Father for His Spirit. In Luke 11:13 Modern English Version (MEV), it says, *"If you then, being evil, know how to give good gifts to your children, how much more will your heavenly Father give the Holy Spirit to those who ask Him?"*

When we cooperate with the Holy Spirit, He gradually makes us more and more like Christ. He imparts the contents of Christ's heart into our hearts. We then think and act more like Christ. We care more, forgive more, share more, help more, and love more, just like Christ loves us. Then we are able to experience the abundant life Christ promised, more and more!

But please be aware of another fact. If we can cooperate with the Holy Spirit, it means we also have the free will to grieve Him. So, what does it mean to grieve the Holy Spirit? We generally do the opposite of cooperate. We resist His help. We don't read His Word, surrender, or ask for His help and power. When we grieve the Holy Spirit, remember what the default is—our sin-nature hearts regain rule! Again, what are the results of being ruled by our sin-nature hearts? Sins of commission and omission of many kinds. Then we possess bad heart contents. We think bad thoughts. We act out on our bad thoughts, and our lives become miserable. Remember what Solomon wrote in Proverbs 15:15 (MSG), *"A Miserable heart means a miserable life, a cheerful heart fills the day with song."*

Questions for reflection

- Describe the abundant life that Christ came to provide us.
- Does the Holy Spirit have a role in our experiencing Christ's abundant life for us? If so, please explain His role.
- Are most Christians living the abundant life Christ promised? If so—to what level?

12

CHEERFUL GRATEFUL
PEACEFUL HEARTS

YOU PROBABLY HAVE heard this phrase before; a cheerful heart is a grateful heart! But what does this phrase mean? It means a person who has a heart of genuine thankfulness is also cheerful, grateful and peaceful. Amazingly, such simple heart conditions can have a positive, enjoyable effect on our lives—and on those we relate to. These enjoyable conditions are additional reasons why we should, above all else, guard our hearts for God-pleasing content.

As explained before, we have deceptive, wicked hearts. When we are led by our sin-nature hearts, we do what is in our hearts. The contents may even include emotions like worry, envy, jealously, or resentment. Needless to say, none of these contents are enjoyable for us or for those in our lives. All four of these emotions do not emit feelings of gratitude. Instead, these emotions emit concerns for being used, disrespected, deprived, cheated, or treated unfairly.

We may worry and fear that someone is taking advantage of us. We may envy someone for something we lack and desire. We may show jealousy because we think someone is better off than us. We may even become resentful or hate-filled because someone has done something that we perceive is unjust! If we harbor just one of these emotions, we can do real harm to ourselves and to our relationships with friends, family, neighbors, and coworkers.

If we can catch ourselves experiencing these emotions (with the Holy Spirit's help), we need to remember what God says in the following scripture verses:

> "What causes fights and quarrels among you? Don't they come from your desires that battle within you? You desire but do not have, so you kill. You covet but you cannot get what you want, so you quarrel and fight. You do not have because you do not ask God." (James 4:1–2 NIV)

> "If we are living now by the Holy Spirit's power, let us follow the Holy Spirit's leading in every part of our lives. Then we won't need to look for honors and popularity, which lead to jealousy and hard feelings." (Galatians 5:25–26 TLB)

> "For there is no difference between Jew and Gentile—the same Lord is Lord of all and richly blesses all who call on him." (Romans 10:12 NIV)

> "And my God will meet all your needs according to the riches of his glory in Christ Jesus." (Philippians 4:19 NIV)

> "Rejoice always, pray continually, give thanks in all circumstances; for this is God's will for you in Christ Jesus." (1 Thessalonians 5:16–18 NIV)

When we experience worry, envy, resentment, our hearts are focused on what we desire, not on the *fulfiller* of our needs and desires. When the Holy Spirit guides our hearts, He helps us see our bad behaviors, and he reminds us of all God's gracious gifts. With the

Spirit's leading, our hearts then become more and more humble and grateful like Christ.

For example—experience for just a moment how our hearts change simply by reflecting on this partial list of things God does for us:

- creates our bodies, minds, and spirits,
- gives and sustains our lives,
- supplies all our needs and some of our wants,
- heals us when sick or hurt,
- protects us from danger and evil,
- gives us talents and skills,
- provides work and income,
- gives us health to work and live,
- blesses us with friends and families,
- forgives our sins and imparts faith,
- gives us Jesus and His Holy Spirit to help us live our daily lives,
- promises eternal life with Him in heaven,
- loves us beyond our human understanding!

From the verses and list above, we see three important facts: 1) Everything does indeed come from God; 2) He wants us to be thankful for all He gives; 3) He wants us to be thankful in all circumstances. When the Spirit reminds us of these facts, our hearts become humble, grateful, and cheerful, instead of worried, anxious, or envious about stuff that we think matters, but often really isn't all that important. With the Spirit's help, we learn to simply trust God for everything with grateful hearts.

A heart of gratitude brings praise, glory, and honor to God with joy, contentment, and peace for us.

> "A peaceful heart leads to a healthy body;
> jealousy is like cancer to the bones." (Proverbs
> 14:30 NLT)

Questions for reflection

- What can cause us to experience a miserable life?
- Why is gratefulness the key to experiencing a cheerful life?
- How can we become more grateful more often?

13

WHEN LIFE TURNS TOUGH

WHEN LIFE IS good and going great, being cheerful and grateful is fairly easy. But when our lives take a turn for the worse, being cheerful and grateful almost always becomes difficult, if not impossible. If we have the Holy Spirit within us, why does this happen?

We can find the answer in story of Job in the book of Job 1:13–19 (MEV):

> "So a day came when his sons and his daughters were eating and drinking wine in their eldest brother's house, and a messenger came to Job and said, 'The oxen were plowing, and the donkeys were feeding beside them, and the Sabeans attacked them, and took them away, and they killed the servants with the edge of the sword, and only I alone have escaped to tell you.' While he was still speaking, another came and said, 'The fire of God fell from heaven and burned up the sheep and the servants and consumed them, and I alone have escaped to tell you.' While he was still speaking, another came and said, 'The Chaldeans formed three companies and made a raid on the camels and have taken them away. They killed the servants with the edge of the

sword, and I alone have escaped to tell you.' While he was still speaking, another came and said, 'Your sons and your daughters were eating and drinking wine in their eldest brother's house, and suddenly a great wind came from the wilderness and struck the four corners of the house, and it fell on the young people, and they are dead; and I alone have escaped to tell you.'"

No doubt, Job's life took a turn for the worst, not once but four times, and unbelievably, all at the same time! Then his health took a bad turn too. The Bible says he suffered boils all over his body. In addition, Job's wife failed to be supportive. She told Job to curse God and die! If all these hardships were not enough for Job, his three friends showed up and spent days trying to convince him of something evil he must have done to deserve all these sudden disasters.

And what was Job's response to all these horrendous disasters? We see his response in verses 20–22:

"Then Job stood up, tore his robe, and shaved his head. He fell to the ground and worshipped. He said, 'Naked I came from my mother's womb, and naked will I return there. The Lord gave, and the Lord has taken away; blessed be the name of the Lord.' In all this Job did not sin, and he did not accuse God of wrongdoing."

The Bible says Job did not sin, nor did he blame God. Instead, Job worshipped and blessed the name of the Lord! Okay, that's not normal! How could anyone possibly respond with worship to such hardships? After all, Job was human, with a sin-nature heart! What Job had to endure was extreme physical and emotional pain! Yet—he did not sin or blame God—simply unbelievable! How could he not blame God for allowing so much pain in his life? In the Living Bible version (TLB) of Job 2:3, we see God's explanation for Job's unbelievable response when He talks to Satan about Job:

> "Well, have you noticed my servant Job?"
> the Lord asked. "He is the finest man in all the
> earth—a good man who fears God and turns
> away from all evil. And he has kept his faith in
> me despite the fact that you persuaded me to let
> you harm him without any cause."

Remember, God looks at the heart of man. What did God see in Job's heart? He saw good. And what comes from the good stored up in the good man's heart? Good. Recall also what Luke 6:45b(NIV) says, "The mouth speaks what the heart is full of." Job's heart had good content, which led to his good thoughts that enabled him to worship and bless God's name. Job's amazing response again reveals how God designed our hearts to function. Good content in will result with good flowing out. Job had so much good in his heart that God said he was the finest man in all the earth, who turned away from all evil. Wow! That was a lot of good! Where did all that good come from? God provides us a clue in the last sentence of Job 2:3.

God tells Satan that Job had kept his faith in Him despite all of his undeserved hardships. Remember, which person of the Trinity has the responsibility to impart faith in us? Yes—it's the Holy Spirit. The Holy Spirit had to be a treasure in Job's heart. God, through His Spirit, enabled him to endure the pain and bless God's name. How do we know this is true? Job is known for another unbelievable statement. We find this statement in Job 13:15a King James Version (KJV), "Though God slay me, yet will I trust Him." Anyone led by the sin-nature heart could never make such a statement of faith. The sin-nature heart is God's enemy. Only a person full of God the Helper could make such a statement of amazing faith.

Now, in light of all we've learned from the story of Job, let's go back to the question we asked at the beginning of this chapter. If the Holy Spirit is in us, why is it hard for us to keep our cheerful, grateful hearts when our lives turn hard? The answer is simple. We stop cooperating with the Holy Spirit.

We default to be led by our sin-nature hearts. Our sin-nature hearts then deceive us. We distrust God. We then believe we know what's better for us than God who created us! Our mouths speak what our hearts are full of—evil! We blame God for allowing our tough times. We also reap the fruits of our natural hearts, fear, anxiety, stress, and anger. And worst of all, we lose faith in God. The very God who tells us he will always be with us and loves us! Who also says in Jeremiah 29:11 (NIV), "I know the plans I have for you," declares the Lord, "plans to prosper you and not to harm you, plans to give you hope and a future."

Unlike Job, when our lives turn tough, we may lose our grateful hearts to our sinful hearts by choice. Yes, by our choice, assuming we are Christians. In the next chapter, we'll discover our daily choice.

Questions for reflection

- What thoughts came to mind when you read about the life of Job?
- Is it possible for us to have a heart and faith like Job? If so, please explain how.

A CONSTANT CHOICE

WHETHER WE ARE aware of it or not, as Christians, we have a constant choice each day of our lives. What's the choice? It is the choice between living our lives led by our natural hearts or by God's Holy Spirit. Non-Christians don't have this choice. They are not saved. They do not have the Holy Spirit in their hearts. Their hearts are still in bondage to their sinful natures.

As Christians, we have been saved by Christ. But we still possess sin-nature hearts until death, just like non-Christians do. However, Christ has liberated us from the bondage of our sinful hearts. We no longer have to be under the control of our sin natures unless we choose to be. Remember, at the moment Christ saved us, the Holy Spirit entered our hearts, and He began abiding within us forever! As God the Holy Spirit, He also has the power to continually liberate us from the power of our wicked hearts forever! We simply need to choose to surrender and cooperate with the Spirit's continual leadership. Recall again Galatians 5:16 (AMP), it saids with reduced words, "But I say, walk habitually in the Spirit, and then you will certainly not carry out the desire of the sinful nature."

Sadly, some Christians are not aware we have this choice of surrender in cooperation with the Holy Spirit. Some are also unaware that the Holy Spirit actually desires to help us want to yield to His guidance. What is even more tragic, some Christians are unaware that the Holy Spirit has the power to change and help us live lives that glorify

Christ. The purpose of this study is to reduce this lack of knowledge among Christians worldwide. Hopefully, more Christians will then become unsettled for salvation only. More will then also go on to live lives useful for Christ's mission to save souls and change lives.

In addition, please remember the role of the other helper, Jesus Christ. In no way does this study wish to overlook or discount the important role of Jesus Christ in our lives. This study is mainly focused on our spiritual hearts and the often overlooked work of the Holy Spirit within our hearts. It seems much of Christianity is focused on God the Father (the Almighty) and God the Son (the Savior) and with lesser attention given to God the Holy Spirit (the Helper). A goal of this study is to provide some education on the Holy Spirit's role, in addition to the Father and Son roles. But why should we never overlook or discount the role of Jesus Christ? The following verses explain why:

> "My old self has been crucified with Christ.
> It is no longer I who live, but Christ lives in me.
> So I live in this earthly body by trusting in the
> Son of God, who loved me and gave himself for
> me." (Galatians 2:20 NLT)

> "I am the vine; you are the branches. If you
> remain in me and I in you, you will bear much
> fruit; apart from Me you can do nothing." (John
> 15:5 NIV)

> "May God give you every good thing you
> need so you can do what He wants. May He do
> in us what pleases Him through Jesus Christ."
> (Hebrews 13:21a NLV)

All three persons make up one Triune God, Who resides within us when the Holy Spirit draws us to faith in Christ. Then all three work together to achieve God's purposes in our lives. With God's help, we not only change for the better but we also stop fearing so many things in our daily lives. In fact, with God's help, we can do all things! How do we know? He said so in the following verses:

> "So do not fear, for I am with you;
>   do not be dismayed, for I am your God.
> I will strengthen you and help you;
>   I will uphold you with my righteous right hand." (Isaiah 41:10 NIV)

> "I tell you the truth, anyone who believes in Me will do the same works I have done, and even greater works, because I am going to the Father." (John 14:12 TLB)

> That is why we can say without any doubt or fear, "The Lord is my Helper, and I am not afraid of anything that mere man can do to me." (Hebrews 13:6 TLB)

> "I can do all things through Christ which strengtheneth me." (Philippians 4:13 KJV)

Questions for reflection

- If as Christians, we have the choice to live our daily lives led by the Holy Spirit, do we also have the ability to make that choice using our human will power?
- What thoughts come to mind when we realize all three persons of our Triune God work within us through the Holy Spirit?

15

What a Gift!

As Christians, we have so many blessings from God, for which we can be grateful. Our salvation won for us by Christ is the greatest blessing. But another one of God's great blessings is the gift of the Holy Spirit. Consider for just a moment what the following verses say about the value of God's gift of the Holy Spirit:

> "But I tell you the truth, it is to your advantage that I go away; for if I do not go away, the Helper (Comforter, Advocate, Intercessor–Counselor, Strengthener, Standby) will not come to you; but if I go, I will send Him (the Holy Spirit) to you [to be in close fellowship with you]." (John 16:7 AMP)

> "The Helper is the Holy Spirit. The Father will send Him in My place. He will teach you everything and help you remember everything I have told you." (John 14:26 NLV)

> "The Spirit of the Lord will come powerfully upon you, and you will prophesy with them; and you will be changed into a different person." (1 Samuel 10:6 NIV)

"The Spirit of truth. The world cannot accept Him, because it neither sees Him nor knows Him, for He lives with you and will be in you." (John 14:17 NIV)

"For His Holy Spirit speaks to us deep in our hearts and tells us that we really are God's children." (Romans 8:16 TLB)

"For I am convinced that neither death nor life, neither angels nor demons, neither the present nor the future, nor any powers, neither height nor depth, nor anything else in all creation, will be able to separate us from the love of God that is in Christ Jesus our Lord." (Romans 8:38–39 NIV)

What wonderful gifts! First, God gives us the free gift of salvation through His Son Jesus! At the same time, God also gives us another helper; His Holy Spirit, to change us so we can live our lives for Christ's glory! He is God, and He is always within us. The Spirit's indwelling is proof we are God's children, saved and sealed for eternal life with God. And because He is the proof we belong to God, we can live our lives convinced that nothing can separate us from God and His love! Again, I say—what a gift! But such a gift must not be taken for granted. Read below what the apostle Paul has to say regarding how we should treat the Holy Spirit: "Don't grieve God. Don't break His heart. His Holy Spirit, moving and breathing in you, is the most intimate part of your life, making you fit for Himself. Don't take such a gift for granted." (Ephesians 4:30 MSG).

Questions for reflection

- Why is the Holy Spirit such a great gift?
- How can the Holy Spirit be the most intimate part of our relationship with God?

- How can we grieve God and break His heart?
- How can we take the Holy Spirit for granted?
- Why should we never take the gift of the Holy Spirit for granted?

16

IMAGINE IF—

IMAGINE IF—MORE CHRISTIANS understood the true condition of our sin-nature hearts and how our hearts function.

Imagine if—more Christians understood the above all else importance of guarding the contents of our hearts.

Imagine if—more Christians understood how much and how often God liberates us from our deceitful, wicked hearts.

Imagine if—more Christians personally knew the Holy Spirit and how to cooperate with Him while living our daily lives.

Imagine if—more Christians had hearts like Christ.

Imagine if—more Christians truly desired and knew how to experience the abundant life Christ came to give us.

What would happen in our lives, our families, our marriages, our workplaces, our neighborhoods, and our churches? Would non-Christians see differences in us? Would non-Christians see Christ's love in us and want Him for themselves? Would more Christians stop being content with just being saved and also desire to live the abundant life Christ promised to give them?

We can only imagine the possible changes we would see and experience. But here is a possible list of the changes we could see:

- Less desire for fame, more desire for a relationship with God,
- Less foolish denials, more admissions of the truth,
- Less desire for our plans, more for God's plans,

- Less concern for ourselves, more service to others,
- Less fruits of our sinful hearts, more fruits of the Spirit's divine love,
- Less desire for things, more desire for God's Word,
- Less time in frivolous pursuits, more time in prayer and service to others,
- Less worldly behavior, more Christ-like living,
- Less fear of sharing Christ, more souls saved and changed lives.

When you imagine the possible changes, there would be a lot of changes for a lot of people? Isn't this the ministry Christ wants to achieve through us—saved souls and changed lives?

If we desire to see more Christ-like changes in ourselves, we know where to start. We start by cooperating with the Helper. We ask the Holy Spirit to work more in our hearts, continually. We ask Him to help us guard our hearts from bad content. We read God's Word regularly. The Spirit then uses the Word and His power within us to enable us to experience Christ's promised abundant life, and others see God's divine love within us.

Consider these final words of wisdom about guarding our hearts for good:

> "Dear children, keep away from anything that might take God's place in your hearts." (1 John 5:21 NLT)

> "Don't worry about anything; instead, pray about everything; tell God your needs, and don't forget to thank him for his answers. If you do this, you will experience God's peace which is far more wonderful that the human mind can understand. His peace will keep your thoughts and your hearts quiet and at rest as you trust in Christ Jesus. Fix your thoughts on what is true and good and right. Think things that are pure and lovely, dwell on the fine and good in others. Think about all you can praise God for and be glad about." (Philippians 4: 6–8b TLB)

Questions for Reflection

1. As you reflect on all of the subjects of this study, which subjects had the most impact on you heart?
2. In your own words, how would you explain to another Christian, why it is important to guard one's spiritual heart everyday?
3. How will you go about applying the heart wisdom the Holy Spirit shares in Proverbs 4:23?

Summary

This book uses the first part of Proverbs 4:23 (NIV) as the title, "*Above all else, guard your heart.*" This verse was chosen for the title because of what the second part of the verse says, "*For everything you do flows from it.*" Often we find ourselves baffled as to why we do what we do. Proverbs is known as a book of wisdom. In roughly a dozen words, God explains why we do what we do throughout our lives. Everything we do flows from our hearts just as our physical hearts pumps out blood to our bodies, so our spiritual hearts pump out actions to the world around us.

God also tells us in His Word that He has a real concern for our hearts. We look at the outward appearances of others, but God looks inside at our hearts. When God looks at our hearts, He sees who we really are. If God sees good content, He also sees good actions in our lives. If He sees bad content, He likewise sees bad actions.

God says we are born with sin-nature hearts, capable of doing serious evil. God describes our natural hearts as deceitful, wicked, and bad beyond anyone's knowledge, primarily because our hearts fool us using a sin thermometer. Also, because our hearts are evil, we can't trust our hearts to guard themselves from bad content. Evil only invites and welcomes evil. Therefore, we need the Holy Spirit to help us guard our hearts from evil. When we have God the Holy Spirit in our hearts, we can be sure we have the very best content possible! The Holy Spirit is not only good; He is holy as His name states! We can absolutely trust a holy, all-powerful God to guard our hearts from all evil, most effectively!

God also tells us He has provided real hope for us, even though we are born with such potentially evil hearts. We can have hearts like

His! We can even become Christ-like but not perfect. We will daily contend with our sinful hearts until death. So how does this hope become real?

When we come to faith in Christ, He liberates us from the evil control of our wicked hearts. At that time, the Holy Spirit also comes to dwell within our hearts and continues our liberation on a daily basis. He uses His Word, which we read, and His divine power to change the content of our hearts to the content of God's heart. Christ is then able to use our lives to love and save others through our lives.

Finally, even though our hearts have been liberated, we still have the ability to grieve God. We can even break God's heart when we choose to led by our sin-nature hearts, instead of being led by His Spirit. We must not take the gift of the Holy Spirit for granted. Without the power of the Holy Spirit, we default back to the control of our sinful hearts, unable to live godly lives for Christ. When we choose to cooperate with the Holy Spirit (and He helps us choose), He not only empowers us to live godly lives, He also blesses our lives with His divine gifts of love called fruits.

A Prayer of Praise and Thanksgiving

Dear Father, Son, and Holy Spirit,

How wonderfully amazing the Three of You are in One!

1. Father, not only have You spoken everything into existence, but You also maintain all things for Your pleasure and our benefit. Among all Your great works is Your plan for our eternal salvation. You loved us so much that You sent Your only Son, Jesus, to live, die, and rise again to redeem us from our inherited, sinful hearts.
2. Jesus, because of Your love for the Father and us, You willingly obeyed the Father's plan to redeem and save us. Then after You accomplished the Father's plan and were returning to Him, You asked the Father to send us the Helper, Your Holy Spirit, to live within us, so that You could continue to work through us to save souls, liberate hearts and change lives until Your future return.
3. Holy Spirit, when You used Your Holy Word and power to convict us of our sins and our need for Christ's saving and liberation work on the cross, You entered our hearts to live with us forever! Now You work daily with Jesus, to continue the liberation of our hearts until You call us home. Moment by moment, with our surrender and cooperation, You daily lead, guide and empower us to become like Jesus.
4. Father, Son and Holy Spirit, as if all these great works were still not enough for us, You also promised and assured us that we will also rise again after our deaths, to live with You forever, in the heavenly home You are preparing for us. What more could we possibly ask or desire of You?
5. For all that You have done, are doing now, and will eternally continue to do for us, we humbly praise and thank You. You truly are a wonderfully amazing God! We are so richly blessed to know You and live for You.

In Jesus's name, we pray.

Amen.

List of Biblical Versions

New Life Version (NLV)
Copyright © 1969, 2003 by Barbour Publishing, Inc.

New Living Translation (NLT)
Holy Bible, New Living Translation, copyright © 1996, 2004, 2015 by Tyndale House Foundation. Used by permission of Tyndale House Publishers, Inc., Carol Stream, Illinois 60188. All rights reserved.

About the Author

Lynn Stuhr is a retired financial advisor. Before changing his career to financial services, he spent nearly ten years in full-time church work as a Christian schoolteacher, a church education director, and a youth group leader. After thirty-five years in financial services, Lynn retired. Shortly thereafter, he read Proverbs 4:23 (NIV) in a manner he never had before. The reading leads to a discovery with others Christians who were also living their lives as he had lived his for so many years. Even as a lifelong Christian, the discovery changed him and blesses him every day. He prays the discovery will bless your life in a similar way.